Scrolls for the King
POEMS, TALES, AND MEMORIES OF MY SOUL

Mya C. Huff

Presented To:

_____

_____

From:

_____

_____

Occasion:

_____

_____

Special Note:

_____

_____

Scrolls for the King: Poems, Tales, and Memories of my Soul

Copyright © 2012, 2015 by Mya Huff.

www.MyaHuff.org

ISBN #: 978-0-9906520-4-5
eISBN#: 978-0-9906520-5-2

All rights reserved. No portion of this book may be reproduced in any form whatsoever, without the written permission of the copyright owner.

Scripture references are from the NIV Worship Bible, The New International Version. Copyright 2000 by the Corinthian Group, Inc. All rights reserved.

To order copies in bulk please contact:
info@MyaHuff.org.

PRINTED IN THE UNITED STATES OF AMERICA

DEDICATION

This book is dedicated to my mom and dad. I want to thank you for the foundation you have instilled in all of your children. You are living proof of the promise that if you, "Train a child in the way he should go, and when he is old he will not turn from it (NIV)." *(Proverbs 22:6)* The greatest gift and spiritual inheritance you gave us was a relationship with Jesus Christ. It will carry us forever. Thank you for every time you have prayed and fought for your offspring. God gave you children and you gave us back to God. May God account it to you as righteousness. Mom and dad, thank you.

Note to Reader:

❖ The following pieces in this book are inspired by faith and poetic expression. These writings are not based on outer body experiences.

❖ Poems in this book may make references or contain passages from scripture. Scripture references are noted at end for the readers use.

Scrolls for the King
POEMS, TALES, AND MEMORIES OF MY SOUL

Mya C. Huff

Table of Contents

1. I Believe Still..1
2. Merit versus Grace..2
3. Staring Back at You.......................................3
4. Foreign Realm...4
5. Acquitted...5
6. A Way of Escape...6
7. No More Tallies...7
8. The Angel Assigned to Me............................8
9. 5/27/2008 at 11:02 p.m. 9
10. Run After God...10
11. All...11
12. Non-Reality..12
13. No Man Knows the Day or the Hour..........13
14. Fond Memory..14
15. Bare and Restored.......................................16
16. Trial, Test, Triumph....................................17
17. Into Servitude..19
18. So Love On..20
19. Before I Was Formed..................................21
20. It Remains...24
21. The Lord's Will Prevails..............................25
22. Who We Thought We Were; Rather, Who We Are...26
23. Judgment Begins in the House of God.......27
24. Broken to Be Healed...................................29
25. Time of Death, Time of Life.......................30
26. What Brings Word of Your Unfailing Love......31
27. The Gift...32
28. Something New...33
29. Say to Yourself...Enough.............................34
30. They See Us...35

31. I'm Lost..37
32. All..38
33. Taken...39
34. More..40
35. He Is... 41
36. The Eternal God's Heart...................................42
37. Get Out of the Way...43
38. Poverty of a Realm..44
39. I Am in Him...45
40. Another Place...46
41. Dying to Live Again..47
42. The Light Within a Light.................................49
43. Write the Vision, Make It Plain......................50
44. Search and Rescue..51
45. It's Already Done...52
46. At What Cost?..53
47. Battle Lines...55
48. Greater than Royalty..56
49. Turn...57
50. Toil of a Generation..58
51. Hidden Wisdom...59
52. Trusting the Unknown.....................................60
53. Carried by Faith in a Promise........................62
54. Still You Are...63
55. Embracing..64
56. For You..65
57. Your Joy Is My Joy..66
58. Weight of Prepared Glory...............................67
59. An Indescribable Coming................................68
60. A Sovereignty...69
61. The Last Say..70
62. Stand Until..71
63. Tree of Life..72
64. Revived..73

65. Love for the Son...75
66. Live..76
67. Only a Matter of Time......................................78
68. Display...79
69. God Thought and I Was...................................80
70. Modern-Day Pharisee.......................................81
71. Finding Myself in You..82
72. A Headline That Never Ends..........................83
73. We Wonder..84
74. God Simply Said No..85
75. He Always Comes...86

My Notes and Inspirations
Notes

Be Uplifted....
Be Inspired....
Believe....

I Believe Still

As we look to You
Though we cannot see You
Let Your eyes be fixed on us
As we gaze into the eyes of faith
As our souls are mesmerized by a glory we have not seen
You are the secret we cannot keep
You declassified the mystery when You tore the veil in two
From top to bottom it was ripped; then it was finished
Every time I hear of You, it's like the first time
Sometimes I ask the Holy Spirit to rewind
Tell me again; I hear of your glory, and I say tell me again
You are never far, yet you are from all eternity
Though the earth seems bare, the fullness of Your love
Provides and dresses men's souls for the journey of temporary separation
A separation that took place at the beginning
It was the very first time God had to search for the faithfulness of humanity
God, as you watched over Israel then and even now
Please watch over me
I search for you; I can hear You moving
Like the mighty throng of any army whose feet hit the pavement of realms I have not known
I hear You moving
Jesus, I have never seen You
I have never touched You
But I believe

Merit versus Grace

Merit is the system that I knew
Then I fell and looked around
In a pigpen, covered in mud
What happened? Is this right?
This can't be right?
Remember what you said of my life
It was like being knocked unconscious
When did my soul become unresponsive, to Your voice?
When did I ever hear the winds of Your glory and not dance in the fields of Your love?
When the earth trembled
And the clouds came
I made my way to the throne room
To rest under heaven's dew
The rains of Your storehouses are like oils of grace
A tabernacle, stones laid by the hand of God
Who may ascend to the hill of the Lord
Or stand in His holy place?
He who has clean hands and a pure heart
I am imperfect, yet You welcome me
In my own strength I could not enter
Your love reaches and pulls me up
Merit is the system I knew
But it was never Your system
Then I fell and looked around
I hear you saying again, "My mercy can lead you home"

Staring Back at You

Dress it up, make it up
Do we ever get enough?
Of broken hearts hiding behind the portrait of misconception
Let this be a lesson
To every little girl and woman alike
There is no such thing as perfection
Every day you put a little more on
Like clockwork at the break of dawn
The eyeshadow and foundation come out of hiding

At night you look in the mirror
With tears in your eyes
As you gaze at the bare you
Not realizing that blemishes are the story
Blemishes are the stepping stones in your journey
The world isn't flawless, yet we aspire to portray perfection

How long did it take you to wash that off today?
The false persona that says, "I'm alright, everything is okay"
Beauty is a gift from above
So let this message lift the weight off your shoulders
True beauty is not defined by man
Look in the mirror, stare, and accept that you are
God's living flame of beauty…

Foreign Realm

Dropped off by a spaceship of purpose
To land on what seemed worthless
Like an alien, discovering the way of life upon this rock
My heart tried to breathe
Only to choke on what can only be described as the scarcity of love

Walking the roads to look upon brokenness on every side
With all of me, I tried to remember
But the memory produced pain
Flashes of the ages of old hurt my soul
I was away from home…

Savior of souls, where have You sent me?
Tried to settle down
Yet each time the ground slipped out from under me
Tried to live as a citizen of this world
This realm served notice I was not accepted

In my shattered state, heaven struck my mind
Opened was the book of destiny
The script of time
Flames of fire, messengers of the wind said,
"Like Christ, outsiders weren't sent here to live but rather to die to the flesh. So be the constant living sacrifice"
Dropped off by a spaceship of purpose

Acquitted

Serving a sentence placed upon men
The bite of forbidden fruit, placed souls in chains
Locked up in flesh, He made for them garments of flesh
Wishing we never knew
What it meant to be outside the perfect will of God

Crawling to the Cross like a wounded soldier in combat
Most times it's not until we hit rock bottom
That we ask, "What happened to that time?"
When the souls of those made in God's image and likeness
had more than enough
We finally realize God is calling us to come higher…to come back

By the sweat of the brow men succeed
People's reactions to the bad things
Are indeed the aftershock
Of the earthquake that took place in men's hearts
At the fall of men

Scaling this mountain until I make it over
Ever seeing Jehovah Jireh in the distance
Sin is serving a sentence, but only for a time
The cross of Christ Jesus is humanity's eternal alibi
We are not guilty

A Way of Escape

Walked right out of prison
Wrists and ankles bruised from chains of the enemy
Christ Jesus brought me out of reach from hell's archers
Looking back, vowing never again

Grace and mercy waited
On a desert road of solitude and brokenness
Your Spirit led me to face what I ran from, avoided, and rejected
A process, withstanding of the test

Provision, my daily bread was given
Finally spotted a slither of shelter
A roof and two walls
The rain fell, lightning and thunder all around me
Grace and mercy ever whispering, "Take the journey"

The final step, transition, back to the courts of the Most High
I smelled the scents of my Father's house in the wind
Aromas of restoration, royalty, and peace
Walked right out of prison
Through the desert experience, my scars were healed
Jesus, Your love led me home…

No More Tallies

Seventy times seven
Every day I held you captive
Another stripe chalked on my heart's wall
With whatever object I could find in the solitary confinement
of bitterness
Until those chalked stripes read unforgiveness

One day I fell into a sleep
Awakened in a field with a barn
Opening the doors
The walls, ceilings, and floor were full of chalked stripes
Like someone was keeping a tally that finally consumed
everything

A fellow walked up and said, "How would you like to reside
here?"
"This is hideous," I responded
He said, "Isn't it? Yet Jesus lives in these conditions in your
heart. You refuse to forgive your offender."
As I fell to my knees
That fellow whispered, "Let it go"

My tears flowed like the Nile River
It felt like the longest cry
Streaming from the pain that was hidden inside
In the depths, my spiritual existence

As I cried, this gentleman called friends and told me to step
outside
They picked up this barn and carried it
Toward an ocean that suddenly became visible
In that same moment, it felt like a hand reached inside me
Yanking out what looked like a black ball covered with oil
Those gentlemen threw that barn into the sea
One turned around and looked at me
He lifted his right hand and said, "Go in peace; they are
remembered no more"
Seventy times seven

The Angel Assigned to Me

You've been following me around my whole life
I feel you sometimes looking over my shoulder
You talk even when I'm not listening
I pray for you sometimes because I know you do warfare for me
I imagine what you look like some days
Even though I have never seen you, I know you carry out your duties well
I'm still alive; you're rooting for me
Some nights I open my eyes hoping to see you standing there
I don't know your name
But thank you for watching over me

5/27/2008 at 11:02 p.m.

The time is now
Wait no longer
It is essential to the Kingdom
All the earth is crying out
The mountains are trembling
The time is now

Through fire shall all things be purified
Sing to the God of mercy
A song of love
The time has come for separation
It's over; the day of wavering is over

Choose this day whom you will serve
For My will is My law, it is life
Hearts, I will search the hearts
Will I find faith in the earth?

Take down your idols
You are worshipping false gods
Empty your hearts
That I may pour in new wine
The time is now

Run After God

He sits by the lake day after day waiting for you to arrive
Nothing ever happens except for time passing by
When you finally show up, it seems He has come and gone
Now you stand in despair with downcast eyes
Asking yourself, "Have I missed him? Is it too late?"

You sit day after day waiting for Him….
You mistakably came to the conclusion that He is not there;
He is not coming
God moves from glory to glory; His presence is infinite
So don't give up

The place of your breakthrough and deliverance
God is waiting for you there
He is calling you; to come up higher
You're searching for Him in the place you once were
He stands and waits at the place He needs you to be
Seek Him and He will be found
The path is clear; follow the road to righteousness

Stand under Jesus', cloud of love
Breathe in heaven's oxygen of forgiveness
Take off condemnation
Open your eyes to the simple truth
He is here…

All

My breath
My sight
My mind's peace
My dried tears, my comfort
My shelter, My assurance
The Redemption of my past, present, and future
My friend and smile
My thought and intellect
My strength, perseverance, and endurance
My foundation, my source of true love
My security of life
My answer and hope
The essence of my forever
My lyric, sonnet, poem
My melodies
You are
The Keeper and Master of my heart

Non-Reality

I close my eyes and imagine
What power is this…a love unfulfilled
Perfection no…there is no such thing in this life
And yet love that is fulfilled erases the flaws of this world
Can something that seems so real be all in my mind?
Yet that which was denied me saturates places hidden from the naked eye

Let go
That time has fled like the waters of rapid springs that flow into the ocean
Now lost and apart from the body, sinking into places too deep for human discovery
Let them dissipate and be no more
And like the Red Sea, much living water surrounds me
Yet what is most evident is that which sank as a ship
That sits, treasures within, yet abandoned

Heart, breathe and be free
Because that time has come and will never be again
Dying to the desire, living for where I am
I arrived expecting
Only to find there was none; it was robbed before I was conceived
Tears I've cried, that little girl lay down and died
The only time she comes alive
Is when I close my eyes and imagine

No Man Knows the Day or the Hour

As You save souls
And wage war on diabolical beings
As You speak in mysteries
As You refine through the flames
As You continue to pick us up when we fall
As You love us unconditionally

When You come back
Bring every drop of grace and mercy
That is stored in heaven's bounty
We are desperately in need
Lord, remember not our sins
But Your compassion for us

Salvation, Father
Remember You said all sins would be forgiven
On that day, may Your faith make You strong
And as You wipe away our tears
May our hearts catch Yours

For one sheep that has been lost and found heaven rejoices
Yet You mourn for every child who is lost…
You long for those not yet found
Grace, Father, and Mercy
You're good; You love us

The Mediator between God and man
Who are we that You care for us?
Yet we are Yours; through the Blood of Christ

On that day, As You judge
Rewarding each man
According to what he has done
Eternal God, remember the Blood of the Lamb
As You look upon us
May Your thoughts ever be at Calvary

Fond Memory

I miss laughing
Piling into a car with my friends on a journey to new memories
Reminiscing on the old ones along the way
I miss getting phone calls at three in the morning just because someone couldn't sleep
Then we would doze off together talking about our biggest dreams

I miss the unplanned sleepovers
The spontaneous sessions of healing
We hugged, and for one night we caught each other's tears before they hit the floor
I miss the random, "I was thinking of you" phone calls
Laughing for hours for no reason at all

We were each other's joy in the middle of storms
And if our smiles couldn't shelter all our hearts, we all stood out in the rain together
Our souls being content was the sun's cue to shine
Broken hearts were held together
By the hope we all carried that life wouldn't always be this way

Some nights were spent in silence in a park, on a beach, or in front of the TV screen
No one said anything
But our connections were louder than all the words in the dictionary
She was the ear, he was the wisdom, those two were the peacemakers, and the list goes on and on
We were family

I miss having fun
In ways that didn't make sense to anyone in the world but us
Then all of a sudden
In what seemed like a forest of bliss, we all went our separate ways

(Continue to next page)

With the days of old floating away with the wind
We all looked back one last time and smiled
We will carry a piece of each other forever
Even if we never meet again

Bare and Restored

My soul was bare, empty
Of all the pain, and also of me
Of everything that I believed made me who I was
The gift was once my foundation, a ticket to recognition
Until iniquity stripped me of what was merely my own strength

I saw God through signs and wonders
Tried to limit grace to the core place where I tried to fathom Him in my soul
Before I fell, I had the essence of the Eternal God, but what of relationship?
My failures were a rite of passage into the realms of Christ Jesus' love
He desires mercy, not sacrifice
My works were the sacrifice that led my mind to chains that held me higher then I ought

Who better to create something out of nothing?
Seven days and it was good
Three days, He died and rose again
Deliverance took my soul out of time, where the flesh simply cannot breathe
Memories of the past tried to bridge a demolished season with new wine…but it will never be so
He pours new wine into new wine skins; we all must be spiritually detoxed

I am reaching for what? Uncertain
Failure was my rite of entry
Because at the end of the day,
Those who enter the Presence of the Most High
Must enter through humility and grace

Trial, Test, Triumph

Through the storm, my heart was set ablaze
Held in the hand of God
With every test, the heat only increased
When I fought the enemy and fell
Christ Jesus said, "Get back up and do it again"

With every blow, it was like my spirit bled sorrow
He patched me up and said, "Get back out there"
Heaven needed me not just to win but to believe
When I submitted to His will, the battle grew fiercer
But my DNA began to change

Until I realized it was not sorrow flowing from me but power
Every time the enemy hit me
It created another place for the power of God to flow from within
The battle raged on until I was unrecognizable
Again Christ said, "Get up"

One Word from God gives the spirit strength to press on
I continued to fight until my flesh was no more good
Physically I was dead, externally defeated
I had no choice but to live by the Spirit
In order to stay alive
God poured living water over me
With both hands, He touched my mind

Transformed and completely changed
Then I heard His thoughts: "I Am the Giver of life"
After examining the internal state of my heart, He removed it
Placing a new one inside; it was pure
Oils of grace and mercy were poured over me

Then the Son of Man came and set my heart on fire
The fire burned its way inside of me until it was no longer visible
I was a furnace
He said, "Get up and look"
I didn't stand in front of a mirror *(Continue to next page)*

But in front of Christ
Through testing and trial
Internally, I finally started looked like Christ

Into Servitude

Mysterious how such a horror story
Transforms into a fairy tale
The rain fell and existence changed
Rare, unblemished jewel from the heavens
Earth granted a glimpse of treasures
Created to shine, to be the light
In a world of darkness
Like a solar eclipse, catch me while you can
Plunged into the earth, dug up by life's trials
Looking up, there is a place from where I came
A mystery…a divine mystery
Searched high and low
Asked scholars and geniuses alike
Only *One* could solve the complex equation that equates to purpose
Even when I thought I had found something extraordinary
God came and totally rediscovered me

So Love On

You decided when to love me
You decided when to like me
You decided in your own mind that I was no more
But I am…here alive and well
For years you told me I was your burden
So today I decided to relieve you of your duties

Don't bother punching your card today
You have been terminated
We are not closed; my heart is still open for business
The thing is, I tried to stop loving you
I tried not to forgive you
Only realizing I didn't know how

You stopped loving me, but through all the rejection
I still never learned to be like you
It is the decision of this court
That you are sentenced to being loved and forgiven for the rest of your life
By one you despised

I no longer hold you in contempt
I was and still am the heart of God
Sent here to push you to realms of love beyond religion
Where sin abounds, grace abounds that much more
My trials made me all the more worthy of love

Before I Was Formed

You could never really decipher when it was yesterday or tomorrow in this place
But always aware when the Father released something new
New glories took the place of time
There was no sunshine
The Eternal God lights up the whole dimension and beyond

I was training for warfare as was custom for all
My instructor was a host assigned specifically to me
All warriors were prepared through knowledge of the things of God
Each test designed specifically for an individual's purpose and journey

Christ Jesus came out one day to see the progress I had made
He was always accompanied
There was always one host on His right
And another on His left
As custom, whenever you sensed Him coming
We stopped to worship the Lord of Host

He always took a special interest in everything I did
Sometimes He would come and bring me gifts (secrets) that had yet to be revealed
Other days He came and just smiled; it was a sign He and the Father were pleased
I always knew I would be a great warrior
For some reason everyone in that realm knew their identity

This one instance as Jesus stood and watched me learn battle techniques
As He looked on, a host of archangels came to the Lord, and said to Him
"Your Majesty, You are needed at once; war has broken out over a particular region"
He smiled at me and turned to walk away
I ran after Him, and said, "Can I come too? I'm ready to fight"

(Continue to next page)

He called me by a name given by the Father
Saying, "This is not your battle"
I said, "Lord, You taught me to fight"
Jesus said, "I assure you that you have never seen a battle such as this; wait for Me here"
So I did; there was no disobedience in this place

Then just before they all went, one of them handed me a scroll
It was battle plans from ages ago, divine ancient writings
He said, "Read it. It will help you when you go on your journey"
Some glories later…it finally arrived, it was the appointed time

Jesus came out with many hosts around Him
He looked at me and said, "Are you ready to fight? Are you ready to be victorious?"
I said, "I am"
So Jesus, His host, my instructor, and I
Began to walk toward that place
Where I would leave that realm and enter the earth

As we approached the gate
Jesus handed me a leaf, just like the ones on all the trees there
He said, "Take one last breath, inhale it; it is extra grace for the journey"
My instructor was also coming with me to the earth realm
As was custom, everyone received a guide

I looked in Jesus's eyes, I saw a love so pure, and said, "I will make you proud"
He told me, "When this is over, I will come for you"
There is a place where saints entered and bared their testimony.
Jesus hugged me; the last thing He said was, "I will never leave you nor forsake you, I will be with you until the very end; I love you"

(Continue to next page)

One of the host took my hand and said,
"Be of good courage; be strong"
I looked back at Jesus one last time; He smiled
So here is where I am now, in the earth
Longing for the day I can return home

It Remains

I learned what true love was
The day I felt like I couldn't love anymore
Love is more than a choice or a right
It is a divine duty, a means to survive
Instituted and created by One unfathomable and unseen

Unprecedented events of this life almost sifted a jewel right out of my soul
How do you love someone who does not want to be loved?
Opening your heart to one who won't love you back
Is like placing your heart in the grasp of a venomous snake
Yet through obedience to the commandment, Love your enemies
The poison is rejected time after time

Knowing the answers to these questions
Would give a glimpse into the mystery of how God loves us, yet we do not know....
God's love just is
But one thing I know for sure
When the virus of hate seems to creep into the flow of my heart
Love beyond explanation is the antibody

The Lord's Will Prevails

Tired of looking through the pages of yesterday
I decided to turn to the next blank page
Only to find it was full of expected pain
It was either toss it out or try to cram my past with a new story

I could just erase what was already written in my past and reuse the same page
But then the past would always be the foundation my future is written upon
This time I didn't just put this book titled, *"The Past"* in a drawer, only to be read again
I saw the burning bush and tossed it in

It is now and forever consumed
And used only as flames of testimony
As *The Past* burned
It had the aroma of deliverance
In the twinkling of an eye, it was no more

So I picked up a new book, looking forward to blank pages to write upon. To my surprise, it was already filled
Looking up, I asked, "What is this? You promised me a fresh start"
A small voice in the wind responded, "It is My will"

All the plans and experiences that were lined up in my heart to write down and do
I had to set aside
But as I began to read what was written, I cried
There were pages of process after process, test after test
I looked through every page to see when this race would finally be complete

I asked that small voice, "Where is it written that I will make it. When is this is all over?"
That small voice responded, "Don't look to rest in the middle of warfare. Fight the good fight of faith. Your victory is surely written…in eternity"

Who We Thought We Were; Rather, Who We Are

Standing in Rome
No decision made seems to be my own
From the food I eat to the clothes I wear
Yes, even the way I wear my hair
It's a spiritual conspiracy
To turn off the power to create that's within humanity
They have already mapped out your tomorrow

Remember back in grade school
Every morning you stood and said, "I pledge"
Be careful who your allegiance is to
It's not an illusion anymore
Like a 3D flick, they have made it your reality
From the drugs, music, and what is labeled "love"

It was fashioned to make a slave of you
Is it coincidence that the majority of all people stand for the same thing?
I meant to say, is it coincidence that the majority stand for nothing?
Our culture has grown accustomed to death that comes through pleasure

Wake up! Look around you
You mind has been lobotomized
Now you're just a zombie, another creative force in chains
A guaranteed consumer of whatever lies they pour out for the day

Does no one realize we only *think* we are living a life with purpose?
Ever pursuing what is only temporary
You're programmed. And just as computer software, limited to what its writer says it will be.
Every time you comply with the societal "norms"
They have snatched you deeper into the great abyss
Now be transformed by the renewing of your mind. Be free...

Judgment Begins in the House of God

True apostles were those like Paul
A humble man who didn't carry the appearance of leadership
Because he didn't have a fancy robe
Repent, for the Kingdom of heaven is near is the story John the Baptist told
His place was out among the people
Jesus went out among the people
Not in your office or the Benz in the church driveway

You got nine security guards to walk you down the aisle
Your members reach out to speak, and you barely crack a smile
Christ said His house would be called a house of prayer
Now you refer to it as an organization, secretly handing the minds of the people over to the chains of foreign illumination…Selah

Tampering with the people's faith just to make a quick buck
When the Law clearly states money is not enough
Faith moves heaven…
Freely you have received; freely give
Merit has never won favor
Yet you have preached twenty-five different flavors of the "be a good Christian" saga
What happened to holiness?

The people have shouted so much they are two-stepping
Thinking $1,000,000 will fall out of the heavens
All the while time is passing by
Faith without works is dead
Don't be deceived; even those who have gone on to glory are still working
There is no dormancy in the Kingdom of God

(Continue to next page)

Few are teaching how to go after your purpose
Don't just tell me to walk in power; give me the *how*
Christ Jesus is the people's IV
Your "big name" or personality is not their dependency
Couldn't care less about your title
Pastor, Doctor, Reverend, Bishop
Some have set yourselves to be idols

You preach a message with a divine sound, but it's infiltrated with diabolical doctrine
The modern faces of the Pharisees of Jesus' day
Brood of vipers and wolves in sheep's clothing
Those who speak from the knowledge of man rather than the knowledge of God do more harm than good no matter how invigorating the message was that day
One by one, Christ is exposing
To others sending forewarning
Woe to the man who leads the sheep astray

Broken to Be Healed

God encourages us daily to go to a higher altitude of love
Seems like every time the heart breaks, it hurts a little bit more than the last time
But even still, make the choice to forgive again; love again; live again
We sometimes look down, wondering why the one who broke us never reached up to say sorry.
Even when we have promoted love and sought peace
Today may God open your eyes
Those who broke you can't reach you
Heartbreak goes from one victim to the next but never any higher
Victims who choose to stay victims circle the bottom of the mountain
While others make a choice to climb and aspire for something they were once convinced they had already reached. Loves Peak.
Those who have broken your heart can't come back for you
They now dwell in the place where you left your pain
You now occupy a place of conquered fears, with freedom to love and be happy
You are not bound by the absence of the source of your pain
Through forgiveness, you are free
Keep climbing.

Time of Death, Time of Life

My heart was an assassin
When You were absent, weren't near
Never have I experienced a love like Yours
Wanted Your love and the love of the world, too

Inevitably it's impossible to possess both simultaneously
My heart plus the world minus Your love equals insanity
At any cost; my heart's creed and cause
Was to get back to You; with that purpose, I could survive anything

Internally I felt like I was dying
Some nights I heard the Giver of life bidding me to come
All I could say was "Lord, have mercy"
I was in a spiritual coma; You were my lifeline
The only One keeping me alive

Nights my heart stopped beating and there was no pulse
You breathed the breath of life into me once more
What others saw as my death, You saw as the beginning of life
Our failures are just a reminder that we need grace

My soul prayed for grace while I was yet asleep
Grace to revive me from the brokenness of this life, from a broken heart
Grace for the hearts I broke, for the ones who wounded me
My heart was like a lion on the prowl when you weren't around
Now meek as the sheep of Your pasture
Connected again to all I have ever known to be true love

What Brings Word of Your Unfailing Love

Good morning to mercy
Good morning to promise
Good morning to hope
Forever forgiven, eternally set free
Today speaks life to the heart
The sun shines down on the earth
Your Son shines through the windows of my soul
I look up into a space occupied by air and clouds in the atmosphere
My heart smiles because You are looking back at me
As the wind blows, Your arms are wrapped around me
Loving me as a Father loves His favorite daughter
The breaking of dawn brings Word of Your grace
It has been poured out for one more day
God is love, raining down kindness for both the righteous and the unrighteous
That all men may know it is His will that none should perish
But every soul be reconciled to God through His Son Jesus Christ
Good morning to Your unfailing love

The Gift

I offered you a moment of my day
You gave me forever
I laid down my heart
You gave me Your life
I walked away…You came and sought me
I humbled my soul; You lifted me up
This is my prayer, a way of life I have
A culture of a Kingdom not of this world
Took me a lifetime to get it right, Your grace is sufficient
You gave it all up so I could live
You left Your glory and Your home so I would never have to
I never have to leave Your presence or the courts of Your heart
My existence is wrapped up in heaven
Taking what was once destitute, now rebuilt
Repairer of broken walls
Make something beautiful out of me
You are the Potter, I am the clay
Till the end I will stand
Till the death and for all eternity
I will stand in gratitude
What ecstasy to stand in the Presence of the Almighty
What awe You are…

Something New

Things are changing, old pictures slowly fading
The view isn't the same
Its takes pure faith to see beauty in an unfinished masterpiece
The world is like a redundant episode
Take this song off of repeat
With my soul I reach for the stars
Hoping a hand reaches back
Here and back again
Packing up my hopes, dreams, heart, and destiny
Traveling to the great beyond
All I've ever known were the familiar spaces
A new road emerges
The sky is clear, yet the rain falls upon me
Saturated in restoration, new beginnings
So to all the past good times, disappointments, tears and smiles
This is my last good-bye
If I see you and don't recognize you
It is because you were forgotten
And replaced with purpose

Say to Yourself...Enough

It's falling down
Cracks and crashes...yet it seems no one hears the sound
It's the sound of kids dying
The sound of a mother crying
All dressed in black
The wardrobe of the relatives of lost souls to a war
Or is it the fight of one man's greed?
Dressed in black, they mourn
Today we ask what was it all for?
Our nation has nothing left to give
Yet leaders have their hands out steadily asking for more
More support from those they have trampled upon
The jails, gas...or maybe I should just say tax
$40,000 for one jail cell, yet a child's school can't afford to put a decent book in his hand
There was a woman who pleaded with the government
Their response: "Ma'am, we understand"
Standing still, waiting on change
Here history goes repeating itself again
Be the change, the epidemic and revolution
Don't be another tree planted in a forest of barely enough
Citizens mistakably search to be watered at the wells of a people who don't care
Everyone is always searching, wishing, and hoping for fulfillment in something new
It's time for us to be the dream come true
Of a life better than this...

They See Us

Servants of love and purity
Servants of grace
Ministers in the wind and flames of fire
Ready and armed for war

Waiting to do battle on behalf of a creation sought after by the Living God
They are looking for an opportunity to unleash the promises of God
To show forth His glory
They stand at the windows of the heavens
Waiting for faith, to rise as a memorial before the Lord
So the doors can finally be opened

On the hills they wait
A mountain with hidden treasures within
Warring host whose swords are ever drawn
To do our bidding
Divine angelic hosts stand on post
Watching over those on whom His favor rests

Divine air strike teams circle the perimeter, expanding beyond the galaxies
Protecting the place where humanity dwells
They are ever watching and waiting
For the words to be released from the tongues of men
For someone to say, "Take this place for the glory of the Lord"
The Lord watches, His eyes going to and fro on the earth
Seeking a heart justified by grace

Angelic host stand waiting for the appointed time
They do not move, but wait for Word from on High
They will march into realms of the earth to gather the souls from its four winds
From the ends of the earth to the ends of the heavens they will gather those God will welcome home

(Continue to next page)

Servants of love and purity
Servants of grace
Ministers in the wind and flames of fire
They are watching and waiting

I'm Lost

With bangles of favor
I once danced before Your courts
My soul mourns
I feel like less than a prodigal son

If I'd known before I left
That time, flesh, the unknown, bad decisions
Would snatch the security of You being my one desire
> Oh to gaze upon the beauty of the Lord
> And to seek Him in His temple

If I had known
On bended knees, I would have requested this last thing
Don't send me away
My Father's house is a memory visualized in tears

Lost, as I walk the country road
Trying to read a map that was written on my mind
I can no longer read these writings
They are foreign to me
Never would I have imagined I would forget
The divine dialect of my home

Flames of fire tell me to pick up my sword and fight
I can barely hold it upright
Like Paul on the road to Damascus
Is someone from the royal family going to come for me?
I have just one piece left
On piece of armor: faith
In spite of all, I believe
That I am not lost to You forever

All

Christ Jesus, today I submit myself to You
Not for who I thought I was, but who You say I am to be
Today I submit, not just my gifts
But rather a broken spirit and contrite heart
Today I submit the agenda and detailed plans I have for myself to the glimpse of the vision You have given me
Today I submit the prayers for myself to the prayers for Your Kingdom to come and Your will to be done on earth as it is heaven
Today I surrender the belief for a better life to the faith that this, too, shall pass
Today I surrender a life of decoyed peace that comes from running from the call
To a life of trouble for the sake of the Cross and the Kingdom of heaven...the place where God dwells
Your grace is sufficient
Today I surrender temporary glory for a place at Abraham's feast
Today I surrender as a daughter and prisoner of Christ
A living and breathing sacrifice
Christ Jesus, today I surrender everything I thought I knew
For the mysteries of Your Kingdom.
Let God arise and His enemies be scattered
You said, "Upon this Rock I will build My church
And the gates of hell shall not prevail against thee"
The day you hear His voice, harden not your hearts
I surrender time in this moment
Jesus forever with You starts, at the moment I surrender all

Taken

My desire
Who sees the hearts of man but God
I see water, living water
Flowing from…where?
Sparkling, lifelike steams of treasures
Holding one in my hand
Nothing is wasted here, nothing just is
A sign from my Father
He has not forgotten
Stand still; He is coming
Keep walking
Enter the narrow gate, leaving the baggage behind
The worker is worthy of his keep
I realized the backpack full of the anxieties of this life
Was disguised by the desire of what I thought I needed to survive
Step into the space
Praising God for the increase
There are pleasures at Your right hand forevermore
Strung together by the chords of eternity
A song of worship, a song of grace
Melodies that were written for me before matter came into being
A song of triumph, victory
It is written…I will win

More

When He shares the good things He has in store
My soul ever longs for more
For the moment in the conversation Jesus says, "I love you"
As a mother looking in on her young at night
You came to visit me when I was sleeping
The next morning, I was not aware You were there
But You are still speaking…
Jesus, I desire to look back into Your eyes
And see the love I have been searching for my whole life
I want to bow before You as my King
Hoping You will smile
And in the twinkling of an eye
Take me to the Father so He can hold me in His arms
Renewed, transformed
Christ Jesus, tell me well done
I stretch my arms out to Him
I hear Him saying, "It's okay now; you are home"

He Is...

You made a treaty with earth
That will soon end
It will wear like a garment
Yet while we are still here
We look up to the stars
Mercy, You spare this place
For the sake of the elect
That you will gather from the four winds

You love connects us all
We know we are part of something greater
When You speak
Like the rushing waves of the sea,
Mighty, a voice with the sound of thousands speaking, yet there is only One

The Almighty has roused Himself from His holy dwelling
Striking down the enemy
Prostrate we lie before You
Groaning, what glory is this?
Majestic over all the earth, Lord You are

Risen, my Lord Jesus You are risen
The veil was ripped
You open Your arms to your children as we rush in
To the most holy place
My God, how vast
Arms that stretch around Your beloved
All glory is in Your hands

Thunder rolls as creation worships
The winds cannot contain themselves
Tears of glory, after the test
Cry tears of glory

The Eternal God's Heart

Let the earth resound
Let creation bear the Name of the Father
As a chosen people
Called and set apart for My will
Seek Me, try Me
The day you hear My voice
I have prepared a place for My people
And all who will come will be accepted
At Abraham's feast

Consider these things
I pray for each one by name
It is My will that none should perish
I know her, I know him
Retrieve My lost ones, Oh Son of David
Return to Me with the harvest
I have set eternity in the hearts of men
Teach them that they may learn of Me
And know My ways

I repeat nothing
Every morning My mercies are made new
I create mercy for My lost ones
I create the dandelions of the fields
Never looking back on what was been
Never recreating, I only create
I created grace

No man must withstand what has been given
Give them grace
Give them the peace that surpasses all understanding
Return to Me with the harvest
I've prepared a place
Enthroned, You shall forever remain, Oh Son of David
It's time; it's coming
I desire to see My people
Robed in majesty and glory

Get Out of the Way

I've forgiven those who cursed Me
I've taken away their sins
They that dwell in the house of the Lord
Remain in Me
My doors are to stay open
Not shut

I continue to search for My lost ones
My doves and lions who strayed
I can't step into a place I am not welcome
I search for a place to repair the broken sheep
I search for a heart I can scold yet love
I chasten My sons to rear them up in the ways of Lord

Don't stand in the way of the lost
Render your hearts that I may start a new thing
If they will only take the heart of Christ and wear it as a shield
I still hear them crying in the night
Will My church rise up?

Render the hearts of the lost; do not keep them from Me
My chosen ones, stubborn
I take My thoughts and place them in the minds of millions
Who would dare to seek Me?
Dare to find Me

I have given My life
Where are the lost?
Render their lives unto Me
I am their God
Searching
I desire to see My lost love

Poverty of a Realm

Third-world countries are labeled for their lack
What others have in abundance, they struggle to produce
Yet it's third-world countries where the prosperous go to make a living
The diamonds, emeralds, and pearls are not discovered in the executive office on the twentieth floor
Why do those who hold treasure rest uneasy?
Reminds me of our world
Are we not all of a third-world mentality by choice?
It's not that we don't have
Some choose not to capitalize on what has been revealed from eternity
We choose to rise and sleep again in the pollution of broken hearts and souls
Water, lights, and food do not shelter the broken
There is a country up yonder that longs to fill the need
Yet in pride and stubbornness, we reject our daily bread
As though we have the right or power to decide if our next three breaths even come
We exist through His Grace...
If they are a third-world country
Then we are a third-realm existence
Because we are insistent and adamant
About desensitizing the human race to life
And to the benefits of basking in love

I Am in Him

Creation is in the Master's hands
I'm just trying to get a glimpse of the blueprint
I have no idea where everything goes
Like the ocean, the real beauty isn't seen until you go deep
Like pearls that hide themselves on the ocean floor
So God is, yet He reveals Himself at will
Plunge deeper into Him

Another Place

My mind's reality was reality's fantasy
What I thought was, wasn't
And what I struggled to accept...is
Does this make sense?

I'm trying to explain a thought process turned upside down
Traveling into galaxies
Thinking I flew straight
 I traveled up and ended at the bottom of that world
And had to be turned right-side up so I wouldn't be walking around on my head

Upon entering, they walked right-side up
But where we live, they would have been upside down
Our norm is their wrong
Their world was full of life
And made our world look like nothing short of dead man's bones
Pure potency, the glory of this place puts every benefit of life on our planet to shame
Fashion...man hasn't even scratched the surface
Because the robes don't wear out as a garment
And every individual wears personalized glory
Wrapped in the beauty of holiness

New foods, and not just a little
Carts of unidentified fruits, these had been set aside
Many dialects, yet one phrase the masses spoke in one voice:
"Glory to God in the Highest"
Souls of man and heavenly host dwelled together, like one body
A Kingdom that can't be explained
No ruler would dare boast of earthly glory at the sight of this
Earthly stars are beneath this dimension
A place where the glory of God shines
This is what my soul dreams...

Dying to Live Again

David, once a ruler of Israel, still a king till this day
Heaven still bears those twelve names
Of the twelve tribes of Israel
Abraham still has honor in all of God's house
Elijah still prophesies
Moses still dwells with God
And John the Baptist, no one greater born among women
Two of these came to see the Savior on the top of the mountain
Enoch left here and went directly home
Heaven remembered...

You have been faithful over a few things; I will make you ruler over many
Is it not better to be a gatekeeper in the house of our God than to rule one hundred ages on earth?
Men want to live forever; is this pure life?
Life hurts, and men see hard days
Men react to dying to the flesh as if they will never live again
What must one do to be remembered, not just by men but by the Almighty?

Our righteousness is as filthy rags
Die to the flesh; live by the Spirit; become alive with Christ
The Spirit gives birth to spirit
To wake up one day, separated from all the calamities and trials
No man can boast of his righteousness before the Lord
Listen...are we not all striving for that moment when heaven utters our name?
Nothing at all is impossible with God.

And I won't seek glory through merit, or the outside of my cup being clean
For He said,
> "If anyone would come after me, he must take up his cross daily and follow me. For whoever wants to save his life will lose it, but whoever loses his life for me will save it"

(Continue to next page)

I have been crucified with Him, and I no longer live, but Christ lives in me
I'll die striving, to make my election and calling sure
My hope is for heaven to remember my name

The Light Within a Light

On bended knee, Father, prostrate I come
Humbly, Lord, I come into Your presence and boldly before the throne of grace
Where is He? Let the heavens open
Standing before the Son, covered in the Blood
Behind Him, doors to where the Father dwells
Behind the veil, You have welcomed us
Father, rouse Yourself
God, hear me from Your Holy mountain
I see hosts shining like beams of light
How can any man be worthy of this?
God of Israel
Rouse Yourself; let the earth tremble

Write the Vision, Make It Plain

Scribes of the Kingdom of heaven
Sent here to record the Words uttered from the mouth of the Almighty God
When it sounds like it doesn't make sense, the increase of faith arises in God's perfect will
Simple instructions: "Write this down"
Yet the weight of what He says is sometimes more than the physical mind can bear
Prophets, hear and speak; scribes, hear and write
Being given interpretation of an Eternal language
Scribes sit in the place where a thing is decreed, where the purpose is declared
Countless scribes, as far as the eye can see
> *"Let this go out to every nation; every people both far and wide; so they may hear and understand My will in this season"*

That One voice is understood from every scribe, from every native tongue and tribe
One only needs to know the language of the Spirit of the Eternal God
Whether day or night, they rise to hear Him speak
Here it's 3:00 p.m., and in that country 2:00 a.m.; in that state it's still yesterday
The presence of God suspends regard for time...
And when the work it finished, sitting back, one says, "Lord, explain again"
There was a time when men possessed the thoughts of God only in their hearts
Eternity was written only on heaven's scrolls
Of what was, is, and what is to come
Eternity is written in the seams
As a garment held together by One promise
Scribes live to hear a message from glory
The very Words spoken in the courts of the
Alpha and Omega

Search and Rescue

In a foreign land, I was captured
The coils of death were before me
Along with others, I was to be struck down
Then a caravan passing through caught my eye
So I shouted, "Lord have mercy"
A man from that caravan approached the line of those condemned
He looked upon my face and asked, "What are you doing here?"
Then He commanded the evil ones of that dreadful kingdom, "Release her; this one belongs to the Lord"
In a loud cry, those demons raised their voices
Accusing me of all I had done, pleading the case for my death
Suddenly that place shook violently
The demons trembled, and everyone grew silent
Then a voice that all could hear but no one saw commanded with authority, "She is Mine"
As He spoke, the chains of all who were condemned fell off
Running for our lives, we dashed for the caravan of Unfailing Love
I asked the man, "How did you know we were here?"
He said, "We pass this way to search for our Lord's lost ones. Now take courage! Return Home…"

It's Already Done

I looked in the mirror and saw the need
Not physically, but underneath
So I checked myself into spiritual rehab
I arrived to see a waiting room full of people
Who were spiritually sick but waiting in peace
To be examined by the Great Physician
When I hit the threshold of the door, though you couldn't see it outwardly
Healing started to hit my soul
Sitting...waiting...watching people pour in by the droves
No matter what they came to have healed
When they hit the threshold of the place, where hearts pursue God
It seems their burdens were lifted, and they suddenly had a reason to smile
I sat wondering what He would say
This center called Restoration is never closed
He is always on call, never takes a day off
You can see the light from under the door as He walks back and forth personally seeing patient after patient
Every time He is in the hall, you hear the shouts that spill over into the waiting area
One after another saying, "Glory be to God!"
It was time, my moment
He stopped in front of my examination room
The great Physician looked, and to my surprise, He said, "I see nothing wrong here"
I looked puzzled...
He said, "Do you still not understand?
The moment you stepped into this place, you were healed
The waiting was not so I could come and do what has already been done, but rather to give you strength.
So you can soar above the clouds
So you can run this race and not grow faint
Go now, you are free...
Then He certified my results with His seal...the promised Holy Spirit

At What Cost?

Attention, those great and small
I will tell you a riddle, and you will know the answer
I had a dream...
In that dream, everyone wanted to be a star
What will you be? For whom shall you shine?
Those presented to you, are they not flesh and blood?
Yet like an athlete on steroids to enhance a performance
Those before you are embodied by the fallen host
Man strives for a moment of fame
The fallen one inside him longs for a moment to be worshipped as a god
Do they not carry the aroma of their father who said in his heart, "I will ascend above the tops of the clouds; I will make myself like the most High?"
You have been deceived
And no wonder, for Satan himself masquerades as an angel of light
It is not surprising, then, if his servants masquerade as servants of righteousness
This world equates notoriety to right standing
All the while they are demanding the soul of a man in exchange for the cover of a magazine
Millions aspire to be...what?
At what cost?
Did He not say, "What good is it for a man to gain the whole world and yet forfeit his very self?"
I saw Satan fall like lighting from heaven
Is it not better to shine in the light of Christ Jesus?
Is it not better to take what the Lord gives than to obtain more outside of His will?
Better the little that the righteous have than the wealth of many wicked
The power of the wicked will be broken, but the Lord will uphold the righteous
Better is a little with righteousness than much gain with injustice
Injustice to the soul, is the present state some of those you hold in higher esteem

(Continue to next page)

Hear the Great I AM saying, "You mean more to Me, your very being is more than science can explain"
But if you would humble yourself, like a child
The Lord will put His magnifying glass over you until all those around you can't help but see you shine in His glory
The Lord Christ Jesus is saying, "Take My provision; have I not promised you what this world cannot give?"
I had a dream
That all men were given a chance at eternal life
But instead everyone wanted to be a star...

Battle Lines

Soldiers have faith in the cause
They have faith in their Commander
Soldiers have faith in victory
Leaving everything behind they take up rank
Willingly, rushing to the front lines
Soldiers leave every comfort behind, in exchange for peace
That surpasses all understanding
It guards their hearts and minds
For the sake of the Cross
They make the Kings joy their strength
There is no fear, only courage and honor
Living to please Him
Existing only to serve at the Kings will
Every soldier lives and dies for the express command of their King

Greater than Royalty

Blessed are those you choose and bring near to live in Your courts
To be in favor with the King of kings
To be loved by the Rose of Sharon
For the Maker of heaven and earth to know their names
Justice, oh Lord, there is justice where You are
Justice for every tear, heartbreak, tribulation of this present life
You have given to each man all they need
To surpass life's expectation
Lord, teach us how to administer justice
Here, now, my heart longs for You to say, "You will always eat at My table"
Lord settle me in the land of those you desire to have near You
How I wish I could remember completely the walls of my Father's house
Are His walls not called Salvation and His gates Praise?
Children sit and wait even if it is for days
At the doors of the place, You, the Son, are alone with the Father
Where You make plans for expansion of eternity
They know eventually You will come out
Accompanied by the Host of heaven
And You will welcome them with open arms
You bless each one…and take them unto yourself
Blessed are those you bring near to live in Your courts

Turn

Don't be afraid; do not fear
I have had enough
The cries of My people come before Me
Like smoke rises from a mountain
I caught a glimpse of the suffering
Will the wicked not be repaid for the coals they have heaped upon my people's heads?
I have stretched out My hand
The wicked will fall by the sword of my Spirit
Countless times I have warned them; they should have listened
And may the calamity they have caused fall upon their own household
I will not take this into consideration; their cries shall not come before Me
Does He who made the eye not see?
Does He who formed the ear not hear?
They can keep their worship for the idols they kept turning to instead of Me
How foolish you have been!
I will tear down your high places and rip your kingdom from your hands
Return, you evil ones, or I will cause you to suffer more than any other nation
Before all you will be displayed, as a stench in the Lord's nostrils
I will rescue My people

Toil of a Generation

Rear up, my children
Who has taken hold of these little ones?
Why have they been left to themselves?
This is not good
They are standing on street corners
I hear the cries of little children; I constantly hear, "No one is loving me"
Why have you rejected my promise?
Did I not promise you greater things?
Are they not hidden in the souls of My children?
Yes, indeed they are Mine
I shall make the widow a mother
I shall make the barren glad
You who despised my little ones will see My glory grow before your very eyes
I will make them great nations
I will make them oaks of righteousness, A City Sought After
They dance before me and make me glad
My daughters are beautiful and My sons mighty
Who do you think you are to reject My chosen?
Have I not poured grace out unto you?
It will only be a short time
If you see yourself as right, then stand before Me and tell me about it, the stench is unbearable
My darlings, my broken little ones
As a lamb that has been left to stray, you have left my children
To fend for themselves in a world not of like heart, that does not consider My precepts
I weep for my little ones
I weep and mourn for their broken hearts
Rear up, my children

Hidden Wisdom

Every man must submit to Me for himself
Every person must turn to Me, and I will heal him
I ask of the harvest
Will every knee not bow and every tongue confess that Christ Jesus is the Lord?
Why do men delay what must come?
There is no choice in this
When I open the heavens, will I find My faithful ones?
I desire to welcome all men as sons
I desire that they partake in My goodness
All has been prepared
Men did not ask of Me My life, yet I laid it down
I offer an inheritance to all men both great and small
Whether Greek or Jew
I bid all to come
I have stored up many things I long to share with them
Seek Me, and you shall find rest for your soul
Does life end with the boundaries of the earth?
Whether lumberjack, artist, or stone cutter
Are there not countless in my house?
I will teach simple things to those believed to be well learned.
And train those who are believed to be skilled
I shall open the gates of my bounty
Rethink, try me
I come
Receive Me as a Father and Friend
Become of a like mind with Me, and you will live

Trusting the Unknown

In the heat of the day
A gentlemen saw two friends walking down the road
He stopped and asked them where they were headed
They said, "To a great gathering and feast"
He said, "Delay your journey; come and walk with Me"
They thought to themselves
One said, "We must attend; all has been prepared for us, and what delicacies there will be"
The other remained silent and then asked, "Where will You lead me?"
The gentlemen responded, "The journey has been written"
The two friends talked among themselves and parted ways
The one set on the feast went ahead
The other began to walk with the gentlemen
The gentlemen led him to a barren and remote place
A place men labeled "None return alive"
He asked, "Is there a reason we are here?
The gentlemen responded, "Rest here for the night, and in the morning you will continue your journey"
The man said, "All right"

At the break of light, the man arose to find himself alone
Yet he saw my footprints and said to himself
Surely He has gone ahead of me; I will follow the path
For forty days and forty nights, He walked in this barren place in search of the gentlemen
On the forty-first day, he was awakened and he seemed too weak to even speak
But uttered, "I searched for you; why did You leave me?"
"Leave you?" I replied. "I led you to a place of greater purpose and destiny. Sit up and eat"

The gentlemen gave him two fish, bread, and water
The man exclaimed, "I have never tasted anything quite like this."
The gentlemen said, "This is reserved for those who are willing to take the journey. Will a hundred times as much not be given to him who will take up his cross and follow Me?"

(Continue to next page)

Startled, he dropped his food and bowed prostrate, saying, "My Lord, why didn't You tell me who You were?"

Just then the gentlemen was transfigured before him and said
    "Is this what you were expecting?
    I search for those who desire to know me
    I was a stranger, and you walked with Me, having no idea where you were going
    You represent a people who search for Me with their whole heart
    A people who will not always know where I am leading them
    But they have the confidence to know I am leading them to the place where I dwell
    My Father's house"

Then the gentlemen disappeared before Him
He stood and saw his country of destination up ahead
When his friends met him they said, "Where have you been; did we not prepare a great feast?"

He said, "I have seen the Lord"
It was so I could tell of His salvation in this land...

Carried by Faith in a Promise

Who would have thought the day would come
When I would have joy in the midst of my storm
Peace I speak to my soul
Walking toward the shore, the wounds are healing
Even though I wait for the chains to drop
What I wouldn't I give?
Let the spell be broken
Let the curse be broken
Let my mind be free
Peace and comfort I speak to my soul
I found joy and a smile
Even though my heart was broken
On a distant sea I ride
Hoping to arrive
At the place where I reclaim my identity
With no answers and no insight
I pressed on…that takes courage
Peace and comfort I speak to my soul

Still You Are

If I never pack out stadiums or play a sold-out show
If I never see my name in lights or hear my song on the radio
If I never get to wear pearls and diamonds or have the world laid at my feet
Do any of these things change who You are?
If tomorrow I cry one million tears, does that mean I haven't conquered my fears?
If tomorrow the sun doesn't shine, does that mean it's the end?
I could go in and out of time
But the clock would always rewind to the moment I fell in love…with the Savior of the world
No longer searching for love, I'm searching for Your heart
And for every new beginning, worship is where I will start
It's in Your presence where my troubles finally end
I prayed to be so many things; now I pray I can be just like You
Taking on the character of God
It's no longer anything in me that makes me who I am
My now and forever are all in You
You always have been, and forever will be
And that's what makes you who You are
You are God

Embracing

Found true love when I lost love
It was my flesh
Anything it wanted seemed to be the best
Of what this life had to offer
It was like a forever high because I never came down; my flesh desired an overdose
Of the very things that manifest death
The wages of sin is death
I created a world in my own mind
The stories of hurt and pain
The evolution of history repeating itself again
Because, yes, everything was the same
Just with a new face
But I kept going back, as if there was going to be a difference
As if today and tomorrow looked any different when I didn't have You
Lived in a world that didn't completely exist within me
Constant battle with myself because my soul was constantly screaming, "Set me free!"
I found true love when I lost love for the things of this world

For You

I write for every heart that's ever been broken
Experiencing pain that could have never been spoken
Trying to diminish the thought of loss in my mind
Of a generation, the hearts of millions
Floating around like goldfish that were overfed
Looking out, I see lakes that overflow with the dead

I write for every boy and girl who never had a friend
Sitting staring at the walls of solitude
There is nothing wrong with you
Others have yet to step into your world
In time they will come searching for something they have never experienced…the greatness in you

I write for the drug addict
Who is trying to escape
For the prostitute who is nothing more than a glorified picture of rape
I write for every mother whose child has died
For every father who sits and wonders why he didn't try to be a better dad

I write for everyone who has a story
They never got to tell
 For every soul who is searching for life's well
In an effort to nourish their spirit if only for a little while
I know how it feels to dial hope's number and have nobody answer the phone
To take a breath and hope that it's your last
I write for everyone who, like me, once forgot
That this, too, shall pass

Your Joy Is My Joy

May my heart's desire for You echo throughout the universe
Until it reaches heaven's gate
Do You not dwell beyond man's discoveries?
Are You not enthroned between the cherubim?
So tonight, Sovereign God
My existence insists on being where You are
As the blast of Your nostrils sends waves resounding through the sea
Your heartbeat sends love rushing for humanity
Love that drowns all fear
And reveals the kindness and compassion of the Almighty God
Tonight let the sun, moon, and stars be attentive
In this the moment the Lord passes by
The wind carries the power of Your voice
The mountains shudder
Tonight, Lord, from my bed
I command creation to write in the sky, "Lord, I love You"
Does heaven see, Oh Lord?
The smoke signal of my spirit
That You have set ablaze for Your service
Lord, the next time You ask the angels, "How is she?"
May the report forever be, "She continually searches for You"
Lord, all creation is Yours
By Your Word were all things made
But look, tonight I left you a message
Written in the stars
Lord, I love You

Weight of Prepared Glory

A crown of thorns…
But You were also crowned King of kings before creation began
Reading this story
Humbly realizing that sometimes the crown we wear in this life is one of weight
But that does not negate the eternal reward prepared for us
The greater the trial and test…
Why, Lord? How many times have we asked You why?
Why does it hurt so bad, last so long?
To the flesh, a moment of trouble can seem like forever
Suffer the temporary, though it seems eternal
A crown of thorns
The greater the test
The greater the reward…that has *already* been prepared

An Indescribable Coming

Lord, I want you to be proud of what I have done
On the day you gather the wheat into Your barn
Please don't forget me...
Sometimes I forget that You feel
Other times I pray that I give you a reason to smile
The laws of creation and the barriers of this realm I haven't figured out
But one thing I know for sure; nothing in all creation can separate me from Your love
So I will keep reaching
Through the Cross, You set my soul free
A little while longer now, and everything will be okay
You said You would be back for me; You said that You would never leave
There were no calculations, no time or date
Only my faith, to believe
That You are on Your way
When this realm knocks me down
I have confidence
That Jesus is coming...a little while longer now
And neither heaven nor earth will ever be the same
All things are made new......

A Sovereignty

I needed You for everything
To teach me how to walk
Though you still rejoiced over me when I could only crawl
I needed You for everything
To take me in when they rejected me
Though You pulled me even closer even when Your love already seemed rich and full
I needed You for everything
To tell me I am beautiful
And lift my chin when I walked around with my head hung down
You said, "Why are you so downcast? You are royalty"
I needed You for everything
To be my protection from dangers seen and unseen
And to give the command to the enemy that he was *never* to touch me
I needed You for everything
To be the Ransom for my many sins
And teach me the meaning of true love
I needed You
To be the hands around my heart when it was broken
And the oil of gladness that wiped away my tears
I needed You for everything
To accept me when I refused to accept myself
I needed You
And one day I realized that my needs did not need You the most
But it was my soul
To be awakened to who I truly was
Before there was ever a need
You were and have always been the Answer
 Jesus, I need you more

The Last Say

You called the disciples
At the appointed time, You called each one
It didn't matter what their past had been or even man's opinion
These were the ones heaven handpicked to follow You
And learn from You
To these twelve, the secrets of the Kingdom of God were revealed
So it is with us
When God calls us, it doesn't matter about the past
Or what men think…only that we are chosen
Those days are the sweetest when Your spirit sweeps through unexpectedly
Anyone in their right mind would stop everything just to hear what You have to say
It means something when we go in search for God
It means so much more when the Spirit of God comes to meet with you
When you're in heaven's itinerary, and God looks forward to His time alone with You
Go now…don't keep Him waiting

Stand Until

We have to learn to fight
Do we not have access to a divine arsenal?
Weapons that are not forged by man...rather the Word of the Living God
Has our armor been given to us to collect dust? Certainly not
Jesus said take up your cross; deny yourself
Should we shrink from death...death to the flesh and every sin that so easily besets us?
We are warriors, equipped for battle before we ever breathed our first breath
He has given us every good thing that every work in us may be complete
Don't faint, and when the battle grows fiercest
Fight harder than when you first began
The joy of the Lord is your strength
Don't lie down; look up to heaven
God is the giver of life
He breathed into Adam the breath of life
So when you grow weary, look to Christ for your second wind
And when you breathe
Use your next breath to send the wind of judgment upon the camp of the enemy
The weapons of our warfare are *not* carnal but mighty through God
Sit hours a day in divine briefings, prayer
Taking note and hearing the General's battle plans for this particular season
Look over battle strategies used throughout the ages
Like belief...that leads unto salvation
Like the tongue...that holds the power of life and death
Like the mind...the arena of this realm that is transformed
Be transformed by the renewing of your mind
Let this mind be in you that was also in Christ Jesus
Jesus wasn't just a warrior
He faced His destiny
And in turn became a Conqueror
We have to learn to fight
Till the death...

Tree of Life

Who was I, Lord
Before You set the world in its place?
Do any of us know how long we really existed?
Were we not alive the moment we entered the mind of God
and He spoke us into existence?
I need to see the reflection that is apart from flesh
You covered man in flesh when we fell
So what were we covered in before that time?
What is my divine story?
This flesh keeps me locked in a realm that is temporary
Yet I'm sure I was birthed from eternity
So, Lord, one more time
Tell me the story
Who was I created to be?
When my existence was only written in Your courts…the place You currently dwell
Who was I? Before flesh covered me

Revived

They made me feel so bad
So I sat down with my head in my hands
Because a message of condemnation told me it was too late
Yet You walked up on me and asked, "What are you doing sitting here?"
I said, "Lord, I lost it all; I lost everything"
Christ, You said,
> "Have you now? Yet here I AM
> Did I give you courage to cower before your enemies?
> Did I give you power for you to sit in a corner feeling sorry for yourself? Get up; this is not worthy of royalty"

I cried out, "Oh, Lord, look upon my land; it is desolate, a rubble of rocks"
Christ, You said,
> "At what point did you lose faith in My power? When did you decide that you were beyond the realms of My grace?"

In silence, with tears in my eyes, I bowed before You
Christ, You said,
> "Do You still love Me?
> Have I been replaced?
> I was your everything
> What enemy has deceived you?
> You are My daughter; when did that change?
> I loved you then, I love you now, and I will love you forever
> I sent messengers for you; I prepared your favorite meal
> You know the one
> Love is patient, Love is kind…yet you did not come
> So I came for Myself to see what is keeping you
> You are never to let the enemy tell you who you are to Me
> Get up; this is not who you are.
> You are Mine"

(Continue to next page)

As You spoke, my tears flowed all the more…
Jesus, Your love would make any being weep
Christ, You said,
> "Will you not return home? Why do you dwell in despair? Does My Father not have more than enough provision?"

I said, "Lord, look at me; what will people think? I need to be perfect"
Christ, You said,
> "Have you forgotten no one enters My house through merit? Every member in My house enters and remains through grace."

Then You opened my eyes
And I looked out to see a great company of heavenly host
I was overwhelmed
I said, "Lord, You brought all these hosts just to come and get me?"
Christ, You said, "You are part of the royal family; were you expecting anything less?"
Chariots of fire were round about us
In an instant, Your glory swept over me
When I awoke, I was home safe
In the unexplainable place…Your arms

Love for the Son

Jesus, we love You
Despite our hard hearts and stiff necks
Humanity is in love with You
Your heart inquires about each one of us
You long to bring us into Your presence
Jesus, we love You
The ongoing battle between good and evil
Between flesh and spirit
And the battles in our own thoughts
Seem to be a cycle
We have only forgotten
Yet a moment with the Majesty of heaven
Seems to pull our true identities out of hiding and from under the suppression of flesh
Releasing the likeness that is You
Jesus, we love You
Your Kingdom is eternal; it will never end
Lord, we will aspire to worship You in spirit and truth
To love God with all our heart, mind, and strength
Jesus, teach us again how to love You
To surrender even in the hard times
To walk up to certain death with hands lifted, saying, "Jesus, I surrender all"
Even if it were my very life, may my last breath to bring glory to Your Name
With hands lifted to heaven
We, the church, will exist in carrying the weight
Of our Father's love
Jesus, we love you

Live

Lord where do I sign?
Not afraid anymore
I read the message that asked
"What will you do for your country, for your home, the place from whence you came?"
I sat pondering all the things I would have to endure to enlist in the company of the elect
Yet I pondered to myself, "Would I not forfeit my life by trying to preserve it?"
But I give my life for the sake of the Name of Christ
In the earth we see the casualties and lose sight of the glory
That has been promised to those who endure
Being surrounded by such a great cloud of witnesses
Should we lose hope and shrink from death?
Before kings men stood and proclaimed that they could not deny God even on pain of death
Trusting God, with no guarantee of tomorrow in sight, only His promises
For they are Yes and Amen
At night men lay awake, giving You praise
Some, bound hand and foot, worshipped You with the part of them that remained free
In spite of their trials
The heart…helps us to escape momentary trouble
Bring us to the place of soundness and peace that surpasses all understanding
They lost everything and were chastised when they fell
But were upheld by Your right hand
When life hits you the hardest, God simply says
Live and don't die
Job shall not die; survive that My glory may be revealed
Joseph shall not die, that My people may live during the time of famine
Jeremiah, you shall not die; a word I have given you
I have given you grace; now speak
Ezekiel, your wife will die, but don't lament; I have a word for My people
Samson, taste and see that the Lord is good

(Continue to next page)

Many are the plans of a man's heart, but the Lord's purpose prevails
Many are the afflictions of the righteous, but the Lord delivers him out of them all
David you shall not die; I saw your tears of worship, may you reap in joy
Paul; stand to your feet, and in three days I will open your eyes for the very first time
Hearts of humanity; remain steadfast
On oath I have sworn by Myself that I shall keep you in perfect peace whose mind is stayed on Me
My heart goes out to you
My Son's Blood is ever before me
I have not forgotten; I have not turned away from My promise
My Spirit breathed upon you, and you lived
Now begin again....
Lord, where do I sign away the rights to my life, hopes, aspirations, and dreams?
Jesus, where do I give over my soul
To the perfection, power, and purpose of Your will?

Only a Matter of Time

Stir up the gifts
Set time by the watch of heaven
Realms move
Synchronizing with the finger of God
I drove Satan from My Presence because of his arrogance
His kingdom shall not prevail against My church
Neither will I dent the time I have allotted him
But I will strike him down once and for all
My children will see their adversary defeated before their very eyes
Look at the smiles on My angels' faces, smiles that the work is finally complete
Be at peace, young ones; you shall reign with Me
You shall reign through eternity…in a place that has not been revealed to man

Display

You called me and I came
I left the rubble of disappointment and brokenness
Spent years searching through the shadows and pieces of the past for a treasure
The appointed time
Separated unto a holy calling
Sitting waiting for the day, the reason I was sent to be revealed
Was it to live, to die, to suffer for the Name that is above every name in heaven and earth?
Fear departs; my eyes look toward heaven
Giving God glory for all He has done
Mighty are the works of Your hands
With a fire within that is faith
Will my life glorify God through suffering or strength?
Released
Longing to look upon His face
God of Israel— May You see Yourself in me

God Thought and I Was

A love song for You
Have I ever written one? I don't know
This place...You gave Your life
So I wouldn't have to die
Yet now I try to learn how to live in the shadow of Your grace
Imperfect...is me
Your strength is made perfect in our weakness
Love me...Lord, love me
But You do...You always have
Love does hurt
It's a depiction of three nails and a cross...innocence in its purest form
Don't generalize God's love for me
Because while on the cross
The Lamb of God knew my name
He called me from an eternal place
He called my name, saying, "Come serve in My house"
Jesus said, "Before Abraham was, I AM"
While you healed the sick and raised the dead
Cured incurable diseases
All the while, I was on Your mind
You knew the mission was not complete
Thank You
For hiding me in the shadow of Your wings
Thank You for what You did
You have neither a beginning nor end, You just are
So wherever that space was in Your eternal existence that You thought of me
And said, "And her name will be...Mya"
Thank You...again, thank You

Modern-Day Pharisee

I saw a vision
Of well-known clergymen and women
Invited to a table adorned with settings fit for royalty, for a king
They had been invited by the powers that be, the very earth's elite…Selah
Little did they know that what was set before them was poisoned
Some died right where they sat, yet others continued to eat
They looked to their right and to their left to see lifeless bodies
Yet they did not get up
Some had seen the very bones of those who couldn't help but indulge in false promises of fame and notoriety
Yet they sat as if they were immune to the law that reads, "The wages of sin is death"
They dined at Jezebel's table
Drinking the hopes of the saints they had deceived
Will God not call this into account?
Does He who created the ear not hear?
Does He who formed the eye not see?

Finding Myself in You

Faith, the currency of a divine dimension
I have yet to see or know
Coming with what I had, very little
But I made the journey
To present my offering before the King
God of heaven, the Maker of heaven and earth
Am I Yours? Do I belong to You?
I desire truth
Which side am I on?
Is my name written in the Lamb's Book of Life?
Coming to the doors of grace that are the entry ways into Your courts
Is this my home?
God do You know me? Do You know my name?

A Headline That Never Ends

I'm not interested in being on the cover of a magazine
I'd prefer to have my name written on the pages of eternity
The Lamb's Book of Life
I shall not fear the terror of night or the arrow that flies by day
Stages are now altars where individuals offer up their souls
To whom? Sometimes they don't even know
Concerts are now venues where individuals hand over their brains
To be washed, or rather put under a spell...they are still fast asleep
Ceremonial whispers of magic, known as lyrics
But they were actually written so you could profess the curse over yourself
Tear down, build up again
Yet like the wind, the masses blow wherever the media goes
Never questioning, "Where has your doctrine come from, and where does it lead?"
The spirit of Babylon is in this nation
People are united and uniformed
Waiting to be told how to think and how to perceive
One day I opened sin's pages only to find they were blank
There was no hope, no future written, so I turned to the end
And it read death
I'd prefer to die to self now and live for eternity
I'm not interested in being on the cover of a magazine
We were all on the front cover of heaven's agenda
When Jesus Christ died on the cross

We Wonder

Thinking of God
All of a sudden
The world becomes so small
At the thought of eternity
The pleasures of this life don't seem that good
The troubles of this world don't seem that bad
Is that weird?

God, I want to hear about You
But they won't tell me
I want to know of the place where You dwell
But they won't speak of it
Holiness, the simplest way to glory
But they hold their tongues
Holiness has become, "that of which they will not speak" in the church
They have turned away from the garden of delicacies
That You have provided, the manna You sent down
Which is Your Word
You are the Living Word
They prefer to indulge in false prophecies
And gospels meant to frustrate believers' right out of their faith
In today's society, they won't offer people the truth of who You are, the only God
Does no one fear that Day?
Is it the world or the church that has turned to a reprobate mind?
Calling what is evil good and what is good evil
They won't speak of holiness and Your Word
Instead, they offer the forbidden fruit of deception to Your church

God Simply Said, No

Ages ago, when God existed in all of Who He is, in all His Sovereignty
Before He created angels, heaven, or earth
He knew the mistakes we would make
He knew we would fall
Yet He still wrote grace into the timeline of our lives
When He saw death creeping up on us
Ages ago, He said, "No"
Not in the moment of crisis
Before time began, He told the enemy, "You cannot have them"
We are heirs and joint heirs with the Lord Jesus Christ
Yet many struggle to accept their identity
Born of noble blood that was shed on the Cross
We make the mistake of thinking God saves us in the moment
When before He ever said let there be light, He told the enemy "No. Not these, humanity is Mine."
Thank God for what He did when it was just Him, the Son, the Holy Spirit, and His will

He Always Comes

Brought up among daughters
Those who dwelled under the wings of Your heart
Walking along the narrow path
You led a great multitude, those You were preparing to present to the King
None that the Father has given You will be lost

Then one day You stopped, turned around
And asked the host, "Where is she?"
Among the great company, there was one missing
When one of Your children walks away, it touches Your heart

Sending forth Grace and Mercy
You gave one command: "Bring her back to me"
So off they went on a journey
Only to find her among a throng of pagans
She had fallen into a deep sleep

Upon seeing her Father's servants
She awoke, but only for a second
Grace and mercy ever whispering, "He is calling you; the King requests your immediate return"
Day after day, Grace followed her, while Mercy repeated over and over, "Come home"

In her frustration
She responded, "Go away; just get out of here"
In one voice, Grace and Mercy responded
"We do not take orders from you"
Little did she know she was in danger

The ruler of this world, God's adversary
Put this daughter in chains, imprisoning her
In a dungeon of darkness, he looked at her
The evil one thought he had one
He thought he had captured another member of the royal family
Sin was the net, pleasure the bait he used to lure the King's children in

(Continue to next page)

Yet Grace and Mercy stayed with her
Even in darkness, there was some light
So she would never forget home
They sent a message to the King of kings
Stating, "She has been detained"

As time elapsed, she sat
Until one day she heard it
She knew the sound
There was no other army in all creation or eternity
That could sweep through an entire realm like a tidal wave of fire
She thought, "My Father has sent more servants to rescue me"

The servants of the adversary trembled with fear; they did not move
Then a light approached the gates
Coming inside, that same light walked down the hall
For the first time in a while, she smelled the aroma of glory
An aroma she had nearly forgotten but still knew

As that light approached her cell
Grace and Mercy knelt down, shouting, "Glory be to God"
As she looked up, to her surprise it was not her Father's servants who came
It was the Son, Christ the King
He looked at her with love in His eyes and said, "Come out"

Her chains were loosed, and the doors were opened
The Son walked her right out of prison
Saying "Go; you are to return home"
Before they left, the Son turned to the adversary
And said with all power and authority, "She is mine"
Just as the enemy tried to utter her faults
The Lord touched her and said, "I see the Blood"
This is the tale and the memory of my soul

May the grace of the Lord Jesus Christ, and the love of God, and the fellowship of the Holy Spirit be with you all.

2 Corinthians 13:14

My Notes & Inspirations

Habakkuk 2:2 "And the Lord answered me, and said, Write the vision, and make it plain….."

Record your thoughts, visions, dreams, goals, and personal inspirations.

_____
_____
_____
_____
_____
_____
_____
_____
_____
_____
_____
_____
_____
_____
_____
_____
_____
_____

Discover your identity in Christ Jesus and be free....

Notes

I Believe Still
Matthew 27:51
John 19:30
Genesis 3

Merit versus Grace
Psalms 24:3-4

Foreign Realm
Psalms 104:4
Romans 12:1

Acquitted
Genesis 3:6
Genesis 3:21

A Way of Escape
Matthew 6:11

No More Tallies
Matthew 18:22
Micah 7:19

5/27/2008 at 11:02 p.m.
Joshua 24:15
Luke 18:8
Mark 2:22
Luke 5:37-38
Psalms 59:17 (KJV)
Jeremiah 17:10

Run After God
Jeremiah 29:13
Romans 8:1
Isaiah 55:6

No Man Knows the Day or the Hour
2 Corinthians 5:10
Hebrews 10:17
Hebrews 8:12
Matthew 12:31
Mark 3:28
Luke 15:7
1 Timothy 2:5
Romans 2:6
Matthew 16:27
Psalms 8:4

Bare and Restored
Genesis 1
Matthew 28:5-6
Matthew 9:13
Romans 12:3
Mark 2:22
Luke 5:37-38

So Love On
Romans 5:20 (KJV)

Before I Was Formed
Deuteronomy 31:6
Hebrews 13:5
Matthew 28:20
Psalms 27:14

Psalms 31:24

It Remains
Matthew 5:44

Who We Thought We Were; Rather, Who We Are
Romans 12:2

Judgment Begins in the House of God
1 Peter 4:17
Matthew 3:2
Matthew 10:8
James 2:17
Matthew 12:34
Matthew 7:15

What Brings Word of Your Unfailing Love
Psalms 143:8
2 Peter 3:9
1 John 4:8
Matthew 5:45

The Gift
Isaiah 58:12
Isaiah 64:8

They See Us
Psalms 104:7
Hebrews 1:7
Luke 2:14
Zechariah 4:10(KJV)
Acts 10:4
Mark 13:27

I'm Lost
Psalms 104:7
Psalms 27:4

All
Matthew 6:10
2 Corinthians 12:9
Psalms 68:1
Matthew 16:18
Hebrews 3:15
Psalms 51:17
Ephesians 3:1
Romans 12:1

Taken
Ephesians 6:13
Matthew 7:13
Matthew 10:10
Psalms 16:11

He Is…
Isaiah 51:6
Matthew 24:22
Mark 13:20
Zechariah 2:13
Mathew 27:51
Matthew 28:6

The Eternal God's Heart
Matthew 18:14
2 Peter 3:9
Ecclesiastes 3:11

Dying to Live Again
Matthew 11:11
Genesis 5:24
Isaiah 64:6
Romans 8:13
Matthew 19:26
Ephesians 2:9
Matthew 23:25
Luke 9:23
Matthew 16:24
Galatians 2:20
Mark 9:4
John 3:6
2 Peter 1:10

It's Already Done
Isaiah 40:31
Ephesians 1:13

At What Cost?
Isaiah 14:14
2 Corinthians 11:14
Matthew 16:26
Mark 8:36
Luke 10:18
Psalms 37:16-17
Matthew 18:4
Matthew 23:12

Battle Lines
Philippians 4:7

Greater than Royalty
Psalms 65:4
Psalms 146:6
Psalms 121:2
Isaiah 60:18

Turn
Psalms 94:9

Toil of a Generation
Psalms 113:9
Isaiah 61:3
Isaiah 62:12

Hidden Wisdom
Romans 14:11
Philippians 2:10
Romans 10:12
Galatians 3:28
Matthew 11:25, 28

Embracing
Romans 6:23

Your Joy Is My Joy
Isaiah 37:16
Psalms 99:1
Exodus 15:8
1 Kings 19:11
Psalms 33:6
Hebrews 11:3

Weight of Prepared Glory
Matthew 27:29

An Indescribable Coming
Romans 8:38-39
Mark 16:42
Mark 13:26
Isaiah 43:19

A Sovereignty
Hebrews 1:9 (KJV)
Mark 10:45
1 Timothy 2:5-6
1 Peter 2:9

The Last Say
Luke 9:1
Matthew 10:1

Stand Until
Matthew 16:24
Ephesians 6:10-18
Hebrews 13:21
2 Peter 1:3
Galatians 6:9 (KJV)
Nehemiah 8:10
Genesis 2:7
2 Corinthians 10:4
Philippians 1:6
Proverbs 18:21
Romans 12:2
Philippians 2:5 (KJV)

Revived
1 Corinthians 13:4
Ephesians 2:8-9

Love for the Son
Luke 1:33
Psalms 145:13
John 4:24
Matthew 22:37

Live
Luke 17:33
Luke 9:24
Matthew 16:25
2 Corinthians 1:20
Hebrews 12:1
Philippians 4:7
Book of Job
Genesis 37-49
Jeremiah 1
Ezekiel 24:15-16
Judges 13-16
Psalms 34:8
Proverbs 19:21
Psalms 34:19
Acts 9:1-19

Display
Deuteronomy 3:24
Philippians 2:9

Modern-Day Pharisee
Romans 6:23

Finding Myself in You
Philippians 4:3
Psalms 121:2
Psalms 146:6

A Headline That Never Ends
Psalms 91:5

We Wonder
Romans 1:28
Isaiah 5:20

God Simply Said, No
Romans 8:17

Contact Mya Directly:
www.MyaHuff.org

Email
Info@myahuff.org
Bookings@myahuff.org
MessageMya@myahuff.org

www.ingramcontent.com/pod-product-compliance
Lightning Source LLC
Chambersburg PA
CBHW070632300426
44113CB00010B/1751